Hillbilly Hand Grenades

Poems by K.W. Peery

Spartan Press
Kansas City, MO
spartanpresskc@gmail.com

Copyright ©Kevin W. Peery, 2019
First Edition 1 3 5 7 9 10 8 6 4 2
ISBN: 978-1-950380-51-0
LCCN: 2019946187

Design, edits and layout: Jason Ryberg
Author photo: K.W. Peery
All rights reserved. No part of this publication may be reproduced or transmitted in any form or by any means, electronic or mechanical, including photocopying, recording or by info retrieval system, without prior written permission from the author.

Peery would like express heartfelt appreciation and acknowledge the following publications where his work has appeared: *The Main Street Rag, Chiron Review, San Pedro River Review, The Gasconade Review, Big Hammer, Blink Ink, Rusty Truck, Mad Swirl, Veterans Voices Magazine, Outlaw Poetry, Mojave River Review, The Asylum Floor, Horror Sleaze Trash, Ramingo's Porch, From Whispers to Roars, Culture Cult Magazine, The Rye Whiskey Review, Drinkers Only Magazine, Under The Bleachers, The Dope Fiend Daily and Apache Poetry.*

TABLE OF CONTENTS

Arbitrary / 1
Ackerman Avenue / 3
Roxicet Ritalin & Rogaine / 4
Danny's Dope / 6
Stud With Stroker / 7
Before November Comes / 8
Holes / 10
Screamin' Your Name / 13
Confession / 15
September 11 / 17
Causeway / 19
His Has Too / 21
Cuttin' Him Loose / 23
Sleepy Hollow Screams / 26
Fried Chicken & Tequila / 28
Bonnie's Habit / 31
Fat Tony's Thompson / 33
Message Of Necessity / 34
Dalmore 62 / 36
Simple Spaces / 38
Letter From The Editor / 39
Nineteen Years & Change / 41
Ron's Riviera / 47
Dog-Eared Worried Blues / 49
Old Man / 51
Letter From The Lost / 54
Temporary Quitter / 56
Brother Ray / 58
Quincy / 59

Splattered Gray Matter / 61
Sexton Single Malt With Pat O'connor / 63
Huston's Humidor / 65
Final Expression / 67
Shell Pink Stratocaster / 70
Quarter To Midnight / 72
Bad Cats / 75
Punk Petroglyphs / 77
Heart-Shaped Frames / 79
Helium Harvest Moon / 81
Weary Eyes / 83
The Other End / 84
Autumn Angst / 85
Barbed Wire Spool Sunlight / 87
Sailor's Noose / 89
Seven Days In Mazatlan / 91
Another Year / 93
Before The Autumn Rain / 94
Peyote Buttons / 95
Aisle Number Eight / 98
Three Skeleton Keys / 100
Inside The Fine Threads / 103
Tragic Beauty In Scarred Wormwood / 105
Mourning Moon / 107
Half Crazy / 109
Konnichiwa & Cameron Crowe / 112
Heroin At Red Square / 114
Hand Grenades At Holy Cross / 115
Poor Man's Pollock / 117

Cold Hands In The Badlands / 119
Corn Mash Moonshine & Mickey Gilley / 121
Shane's 68 Skylark / 123
Another Year Or Two / 125
Last Call From The Bad Luck Bar / 127
Grace / 129
Tailwind / 132
Pinot Lips / 134
Afterburners Glow / 136
Scraps Of Our Hellbound Souls / 140
Chrysler Avenue / 141
Room 206 / 144
Outside Those Static Lines / 146
Gory Details / 148
Thompson Gun / 150
The Tenderloin Room / 153
Trial Horse / 155
Fighting Cock & Rolling Rock / 157
Ezine Anxieties / 159
Chain Smokin' Deathbed / 163
Assassin's Toupee / 166
Bluesmen In Buffalo / 168
How This Trip Ends / 170
Inconsequential / 173
Sunrise On Ko Samui / 175
Another Sunrise / 177
Rhode Island Red / 179
Johnny's Last Ride / 180
Preferred Rendezvous / 182
Peacockin' Poet From Poughkeepsie / 184
Hawk Flop Tsunami / 186

Hillbilly Hand Grenades

This book is for Mom & Dad

ARBITRARY

I wasn't
really raised
to follow
arbitrary
rules...
or concede
to the
greed
that drives
so many
goddamn
sheep
to slaughter...

Ya know..
I can
certainly
recognize
cannon fodder
when I
see it...

And
will do
my best

to protest
inside the
rhyme...
where
I know
I'll be
just fine...

Because
those rich ass
sons a bitches
aren't smart
enough
to read
between
my crooked
lines
anyway

ACKERMAN AVENUE

In that
three-bedroom
bungalow
off Ackerman
Avenue...
we would
sprawl out
sideways
while smokin'
clove cigarettes
on our
brand new
baby blue
queen size
sleeper sofa...

Listenin' to
short bursts
of drive-by
gunfire...
over
Two Bit
Monsters
on vinyl...
knowin'
we were
never really
normal
to begin
with

ROXICET RITALIN & ROGAINE

In my
Roxicet
riddled
twenties...
I carried
a nickel-plated
hand cannon
in my
left vest
pocket
and spiked
brass knuckles
in my
steel-toed
boots...

In my
Ritalin
ravaged
thirties...
I drove a
silver smoke
Cadillac
way too
fuckin' fast
to remember

all those
enemies
I left
for dead
along the
roadside...

Now...
in my
hip-fractured
forties...
I just
douse
my scalp
in Rogaine...
sip this
damn white
lightnin'...
and try hard
to remember
exactly how
bad it got
before my
wheels
flew
off

DANNY'S DOPE

We were
countin'
our take
in room
number
eight
at the
Tic Tock Motel
in Taylor...

When Jack
slid a sack
of snowball
in the center
of the
side table
and said...

*This is
the dope
Danny failed
to deliver
in Laddonia...
we'll have to
roll the
dead man's
dice...
to determine
who goes
next*

STUD WITH STROKER

The night
I met
Monica
at Mongo's
Planet
in Memphis...
she was
still drivin'
her ex-husband's
sapphire blue
Lincoln
Continental...
So we
took it
on a little
joy ride
out to
Jackson...
just to play
stud poker
with Stroker
Ace
at the
Red Dog
Saloon

BEFORE NOVEMBER COMES

In
the midst
of this
Monday
mornin'
meltdown...
I think
of all
the things
I should've said
weeks ago...

That
I'm sure
you already
know...
but deserve
to hear
again...

Like...
I'm sorry...
I'm embarrassed...
I'm desperate...
I'm thirsty...
I'm tired...
I'm afraid...
I'm dyin'...
I'm alone...

Here
in the
shadows
of the
September
gallows...
where men
like me
attempt to
hide from
the reality
of failure...

And
try to
survive
the hangman's
noose...
before
November
comes
to claim
what's left
of this
hardened n'
shell-shocked
soul

HOLES
(For my brother James Dennis Casey IV)

Whitetail
liver
in
a
cast
iron
pan...
with
the
smell
of
a
kill
still
on
my
hands...

It's
Death
Wish
coffee
and
heavy
cream...
gettin'
stoned
inside

for
these
muffled
screams...

There's
a
Yellowboy
lever
and
a
Smith
.44...
ready
to
do
what
they've
done
before...

So
come
on
n'
try
me...
and
ya
better
not
miss...

cause
I'll
fill
you
with
holes
ya
ole
son
of
a
bitch

SCREAMIN' YOUR NAME

I've
been
screamin'
your
name...
up
here
on
the
hill...

Where
a
shallow
grave
holds...
more
than
I
meant
to
kill...

Now
this
ole
pick
and
shovel...

are
done
movin'
dirt....

So
I
wrapped
my
good
knife...
in
what's
left
of
my
shirt...
Yeah...
I'm
screamin'
your
name...

And
I'm
done
movin'
dirt

CONFESSION

Judge Kellogg
had issued
a bench
warrant
for my
arrest...
for failure
to appear...
on the
same mornin'
the Twin Towers
fell...

And
as I
watched
it all
unfold...
from that
tiny square
window
in my
holding
cell...

I remember
thinkin'...

As soon
as I
make
bail...
I'm gonna
leave this
jail...
and go
straight
to
confession

SEPTEMBER 11

On
September 11
2001...
I sat
in the sun
on the
fourth step
at St. Mary's
Catholic Church...
anxiously awaitin'
Father Tom's
return...

I needed
him to hear
my overdue
confession...
and was
willin' to wait
as long as
it took
to get
shit
off my
chest...

I wanted
to come
clean...
before
tryin' to
re-enlist
in Kansas City
the next
mornin'

CAUSEWAY

I
ride
along...
this
ole
causeway
alone...

Searchin'
for
somethin'...
to
rattle
these
bones...

Past
forty
five...
feelin'
damn
near
sixty...

Where
my
sufferin'
fades...
and
the
truth
forgives
me

HIS HAS TOO

We
were
just
shootin'
the
shit
out
in
Carl's
garage...
the
afternoon
his
wife
Faye
passed
away...

And
every
day
since
her
ole
heart

stopped
beatin'...
I'm
goddamn
certain
his
has
too

CUTTIN' HIM LOOSE

When
we
found
Carl
on
New
Year's
Day
in
Ninety
Two...

His
head
was
twice
its
normal
size...
in
that
fuckin'
noose...

And
while
we

waited
for
the
coroner...
before
cuttin'
him
loose...

I
noticed
one
of
his
Red
Wing
boots...

had
made
its
way
to
the
greasy
garage
floor
already...

As
George
Jones
sang
an
old
Tom
T.
song
on
the
brand
new
workbench
radio
I
gave
him
for
Christmas

SLEEPY HOLLOW SCREAMS

The
night
Bobby
Ray
shot
his
step
son
in
the
face
at
Andy
B's
in
Bartlett
Tennessee...

You
could
hear
his
Mama's
bloodcurdlin'
screams...

all
the
way
over
at
my
place
off
Sleepy
Hollow
Road

FRIED CHICKEN & TEQUILA

I
just
heard
John
Prine
say...
the
best
thing
about
recordin'
with
Dave
Cobb
at
RCA...
was
the
good
fried
chicken
and
top
shelf
tequila...

And
I'm
really
not
that
surprised
to
hear
him
say
it...

Because
most
of
the
best
Americana
scribes...

have
come
to
realize...

Even
the
cheapest
tequila...
and

bad
fried
chicken...
are
better
than
dependin'
on
a
fad
religion...

Or
the
more
expensive
things...
desperate
writers
try
to
do...
to
just
get
by

BONNIE'S HABIT

Bonnie
likes to
day drink
down
at Joe's...
and
shoot
her big
mouth
off
about
Cindy's
clothes...
Tammy's
tattoos...
n' Brenda's
new boyfriend...

It's really
kinda sad
to hear
her say
such shitty
things
about her
so-called
friends...

And
Buckshot
says
he thinks
Bonnie is
near the end...
n' jealous
of all the
neighborhood girls
that done
made good...
without
havin' to
work the
streets
six nights
a week

just to
feed
the
habit

FAT TONY'S THOMPSON

They
were up
playin' Spades
in room 268...
at the
Madison Hotel
in Memphis...

N' as
Red Lane
sang..
Blackjack
County
Chain...

A strange
knock came...

Causin'
their luck
to change...

Just
seconds before...
they opened
the door...
and Fat Tony
went to work
with his
Thompson

MESSAGE OF NECESSITY

A message
of necessity...

To the
pasty-faced
pseudo-intellectual
who keeps tryin'
to snipe at me
from behind
his privacy
screen...

I'm
still here...

Flashin' ya
this crooked
middle finger...

N' rest assured...
there's no
distance
too great
for me
to reach
you...

And
I'll do it
from the comfort
of my plush
velvet couch
in Kansas City...
motherfucker

DALMORE 62

When
Madsen
called
me
from
the
Cloakroom
Bar
in
Montreal
late
last
night...

He
said
he'd
been
itchin'
for
a
goddamn
fight...

But

decided
to
settle
for
a
dram
of
Dalmore
62
instead

SIMPLE SPACES

Shaver
always says —
*Simplicity
doesn't need
to be greased...*

And for
the most part
I would agree...

Because
somewhere
in between...

All the
common words
we lean on...

Are the
open-ended
spaces...

We
sometimes
need...

Just to
let our
consciousness
breathe

LETTER FROM THE EDITOR

I
received
an abbreviated
letter
from the
editor
this
afternoon...

It says —
Thanks
for your
recent
submission
to our
world-class
literary magazine...

While
what
you sent
is not
the worst work
we've ever
seen....

It's just not
a fit...
with the

*preferred brand
of horseshit
we're dedicated
to publishing
here...*

*Please wait
a minimum
of 90 days
before
resubmitting...
so we can
ignore your
dumb ass*

*for at least
another
6 months...*

*And
try harder
to make
you think...
we actually
take what
you do
seriously...
knowing
full well
we never
will*

NINETEEN YEARS & CHANGE

I've
been
a
Registered
Nurse
now
for
nineteen
years
and
change...

And
still
feel
helpless...
when
someone
I
know
gets
sick
or
injured...

It
drives
me
a
little
insane...
n'
makes
me
wish
I
didn't
understand
all
of
the
possibilities...

Ya
know
I've
held
hands
with
the
angel
of
death

so
many
times...
that
words
are
no
longer
necessary...

My
emotions
are
buried
so
deep
in
this
virtual
cemetery...
who
really
knows
if
or
when
I'll
ever
feel
again...

Yeah...
I've
been
a
Registered
Nurse
now

for
nineteen
years
and
change...

So
when
you
see
the
tears
well
up
in
my
big
brown
bloodshot
eyes...

Please
know
our
souls
are
somehow
synchronized...
and
that
I'll
never
stop
searchin'
for
a
way
to
save
you...

And
save
me...

From
what's
waitin'
patiently...

out
in
the
wings
for
both
of
us

RON'S RIVIERA

When
the
rookie
State
Trooper
rolled
up
on
Ron's
Riviera
at
mile
marker
123...

It
had
already
been
torched...

And
his
well
charred
corpse

was
still
smolderin'
in
the
driver's
seat

DOG-EARED WORRIED BLUES

There's a
dog-eared
whiskey label
still clingin'
to the bottle
I've been
sippin' on
since three
this afternoon...

And
even if
I could find
a cleaner way
to heal
some of these
ole wounds...

I'm not
too damn sure
it would
do me
any good...

So I'll
just sit here
n' sip...
while
listenin'
to Skip
sing
more
of the
Worried Blues

OLD MAN

I
met
an
old
man
in
the
mirror
this
mornin'...
n'
he
reminded
me
of
my
late
Granddad...

And
it's
goddamn
sad
to
think
he's

been
gone
so
long...
I've
somehow
forgotten
most
of
the
sage
advice
he
tried
to
share
with
me...

Not
that
I
was
ever
really
payin'
close
attention
or

listenin'
as
much
as
he
wanted
me
to....

But
I
sure
as
hell
shoulda
been

LETTER FROM THE LOST

This
letter
from
the
lost
is
not
meant
to
be
an
apology...

Just
an
acknowledgement...
that
I
still
feel
you
here
with
me...

Especially
on
nights

like
these...
when
I'm
down
on
bended
knee....

Prayin'
for
one
final
reprieve...
or
anything

to
delay
what
I
know
I
have
comin'
soon

TEMPORARY QUITTER

I
gave up
drinkin'
again today...
And
buried
my bottles
in an
unmarked
grave...

Been
here before...
when
my soul
needed saved...
Just
a temporary
quitter...
ridin'
delta waves
Yeah...
I'm a
temporary
quitter...
ridin'
delta waves

I
gave up
weed
again today...
But
I'm farmin'
this patch...
it's a
medicinal strain...

Like
Uncle Willie
says...
no pain's
the same...
I'm
a temporary
quitter...
ridin'
delta waves...
Just
a temporary
quitter...
ridin'
delta waves

BROTHER RAY
(For Ray Charles)

In a 1953 interview
Ray Charles said —

*Not one drop
of my self-worth
depends on your
acceptance of me*

And the rest
is history…

Because
Brother Ray
went on
to play
for more than
six decades

He defied
all the rules…

Blending
soul, country,
jazz & blues

And his
influence
will live on
forever

QUINCY
(For Q)

A wise man
named Quincy
once told me
an ego is just
overdressed
insecurity...

He said —
Kid...
you need
to learn
to shut
your fuckin'
mouth...
n' listen
to what
smarter
folks are
attemptin'
to give you
for free....

And if
you still have
unanswered
questions —
call me....

He then
went on
to say —
*From birth
to death...
the average person
only gets
27,000 days*

*It's all
up to you
young hustler...*

*Will ya
reassess
your essence
on the regular...
or succumb
too soon
to what's waitin'
on the valley floor*

SPLATTERED GRAY MATTER

Is honesty
really
the best
policy...
when everyone
already knows
you're
a goddamn
liar...

Like a
wise man
from Waco
once said —
Never play
Russian roulette
with an
automatic ....

Sure...
the cold
hard truth
might set
ya free...

But the
odds are
certainly
against
a misfire...

And
what kind of
sick son of a bitch
gets his kicks
scoopin' up
the splattered
gray matter
of a lyin' man
anyway

SEXTON SINGLE MALT WITH PAT O'CONNOR

At
the
tail
end
of
an
eight
day
bender…
she
found
me
down
at
Norty's…
just
slow
sippin'
Sexton
single
malt
with
Pat
O'Connor…

Tryin'
to
work
up

enough
courage
to
ask
him
how
it
felt
when
he
lost
the
title
to
Buddy
Rogers
at
Comiskey
Park
in
June
of
'61

HUSTON'S HUMIDOR
(For John Huston)

Huston
had
an
antique
burl
wood
cigar
humidor…
situated
at
an
angle …
on
his
two-
sided
art
deco
desk…

The
custom
engraved
plate
said —
Lucky knows
how to find me…
here on Franklin Avenue…

And
one
could
surmise
it
was
his
most
prized
possession…

besides
the
framed
love
letter
he'd
received
from
Barbara
Bouchet…
just
seven
days
after
the
wrap
party
for
Casino
Royale
in
London

FINAL EXPRESSION

Somewhere
inside
this
wicked
November
wind…
I
found
evidence
of
a
so-
called
friend...

Abandoned
behind
the
Twin
City
Tavern…
like
a
four
door

Plymouth
Fury
with
a
blown
head
gasket...

Yeah —
we
all
knew...
that
ole
sick
son
of
a
bitch

wasn't
too
scared
of
dyin'
ugly...

And
this
time
around
his
final
expression
was
more
peaceful…
mainly
because
he
didn't
have
to
pull
the
trigger
himself

SHELL PINK STRATOCASTER
(For Tony Joe White)

There's
an old
diamondback strap
still attached
to that cracked
shell pink
Stratocaster
he left
on stage
the last time
he played
at Red's Lounge
down in
Clarksdale...

And as
Rich Woman Blues...
bleeds warm
straight through...
that ole
Fifty-Seven
Seeburg
in back...

I know
the Swamp Fox
is gone...
but his
spirit
lives on...
in those
songs
that'll move
mountains
forever

QUARTER TO MIDNIGHT

At
half
past
eleven
I
noticed
your
brand
new
sharkskin
suit
swing
dancin'
with
a
clone
to
Brigitte
Bardot…

I
was
staked
out
inside
the
cottonwood
shadows…
in

booth
number
three
at
the
Green
Lady
Lounge....

Waitin'
for
The
Stones
to
stop
singin'

*Down
the Road
Apiece...*
just
long
enough
to
engage
the
grease
on
my
slide

N'
let
those
goddamn
hollow
points
fly...
before
sayin'
goodbye...
one
final
time...
at
a
quarter
to
midnight

BAD CATS

Kosher
Kush
on a
Coltrane
night...
just eatin'
my smoke
in the
blue
moonlight...

There's a
cone top
two slat
in clearspring
green...
next
to Mama's
old sewin'
machine...

It's
already
autumn
n' this
flannel
feels good...

sippin'
three fingers
of Blanton's
from some
charred
oak wood...

Been ridin'
big waves
in this
blue livin'
room...
where all
the bad
cats jam...
then leave
too soon

PUNK PETROGLYPHS

We
were
slow
trollin'
down
Rock
Crusher
road...
in
my
'93
Eldorado...

When
ol'
Hog
Head
said...

Let's
take
this
bottle
of
Booker's

to
the
base
of
Piney
Creek
Ravine...

Just
to
see
how
obscene
those
punk
petroglyphs
get
after
sunset

HEART-SHAPED FRAMES

It's
ninety-
nine
smiles
from
here
to
the
truth...
where
purgatory
tongues
taste
eternal
youth...

Like
a
jet
black
Caddy
with
faint
phantom
flames...

or
three-
card
Monte
wearin'
heart-
shaped
frames

HELIUM HARVEST MOON

Under
a
helium
harvest
moon...
I
sketched
her
frown
in
a
sugar
spoon...

As
warm
red
candle
wax...
pooled
inside
the
sidewalk
cracks...

Near
the
side
entrance
at
Guardian
Angels
Parish
down
in
Westport

WEARY EYES

We'd been
snortin'
lines of
angel dust
off a
Blacksmith's
anvil...
just
moments
before...
they
kicked in
our door...
with a
federal
search
warrant
and the
weary eyes
of an
executioner

THE OTHER END

On the other end
Of this crooked line
Is a story so sad
You'd think it's mine
Where drugs n' booze
Still eat their young
On the other end
Of this kettle drum –

On the other end
Of this Hell we breathe
Agin' eighteen years
In less than three
Where sex n' shame
Sell our souls too cheap
On the other end
With those secrets we keep –

On the other end
Of every hollow shell
Is a skeleton key
And a wishin' well
Where the sheep get slaughtered
And stone streets run red
On the other end
Of what's in our heads

Yeah...
The other end...
Of what's in our heads

AUTUMN ANGST

There's a
burnt orange dahlia
sippin' warm red wine
from a champagne flute
with rhinestone sides

Her third eye's
missin'....
she's gotta gun
on her hip
Yeah…there's a
burnt orange dahlia
with death
on her lips
Oh…
She's the
burnt orange dahlia…
with death
on her lips —

There's a
black-eyed Susan
with a shit-eatin' grin
scarrin' my heart
where the dead end….
ends

Her left hand's
steady...
when she
needs it to be
Yeah...ole
black-eyed Susan's
carvin' snakes
on me
Cause...ole
black-eyed Susan
loves makin' me
bleed

BARBED WIRE SPOOL SUNLIGHT

This
barbed
wire
spool
sunlight
makes
my
bloodshot
eyeballs
itch…

And
I'm
not
gonna
quit…
till
we
find
that
greedy
son
of
a
bitch...

Hidin'
out
on
a
Banana
Boat
beach
somewhere
in
Southern
California....

Spendin'
what's
left
of
the
stolen
scratch....
he's
still
not
certain
he
got
away
with

SAILOR'S NOOSE

As I
pour
another
inside
this blue
I try
to hide
n' think less
of
you...

It's
isolated
words
on superfine
white
And the
reflection
of surrender
in my
desk lamp light —

Where gin
drowns
guilt
over

Iowa ice
I trace
your lips...
then
taste them
twice...

This
suicide note's..
wearin'
blue suede
shoes....
Like
poetic license
in a
sailor's
noose

SEVEN DAYS IN MAZATLAN

After
we
paid
our
one-
eyed
wheelman
and
that
sketchy
shade
tree
surgeon
off
Springdale
drive...

We
split
eighty
five
large
three
ways
and
spent

seven
days
at
The
Palms
down
in
Mazatlan

Just
lickin'
our
wounds...
while
tryin'
to
dream
up
a
better
way
to
do
things
the
next
time
around

ANOTHER YEAR

As
I
watched
a
mature
twelve
pointer...
tend
his
scrapes
along
the
East
edge
of
Buckshot
Draw...

I
admired
his
relentless
approach...
despite
the
rut
and
let
him
go
another
year

BEFORE THE AUTUMN RAIN

In
the
thick
gravel
dust
on
his
midnight
black
Silverado
hood...
he
would
make
detailed
diagrams...
in
a
last-
ditch
attempt
to
illustrate
his
final
wishes
before
the
Autumn
rain
set
in

PEYOTE BUTTONS

We
were
chewin'
peyote
buttons
on
the
outskirts
of
Area
51...

When
a
pyrotechnic
energy
washed
over
me...
like
the
tidal
beauty
at
The
Bay
of
Fundy...

Or
a
Milky
Way
trip
over
Joshua
Tree
in
January...

Where
everything
connected
entirely...

and
I
forgave
openly...
because
fear
fueled
hate
no
longer
mattered...

And
my
hillbilly
soul
somehow
remembered
it
never
did

AISLE NUMBER EIGHT

This
mornin'
in
aisle
number
eight...
it
dawned
on
me...

That
a
dyin'
man
really
has
no
need
for
the
Value
Pack
Old
Spice
Swagger
deodorant...

Because
he'll
be
feedin'
those
oxeye
daisies...
long
before
the
real
stink
sets
in

THREE SKELETON KEYS

There
were
three
skeleton
keys
on
a
gas
station
ring...
hangin'
just
inside
the
chestnut
kitchen
door
at
my
Grandpa's
home
place...

One
went
to

the
main
smokehouse
door...

The
second
to
a
spooky
ass
root
cellar...

And
the
third...

to
a
whitewashed
tool
trunk...

That
was
situated
next
to

an
old
tin
shed...
Grandpa
built
with
his
brother
Carl...
after
they
somehow
survived
the
Second
World
War

INSIDE THE FINE THREADS

Inside the
fine threads
of every lie
I weave...
Are unspoken
words
I dare not
breathe...
Like the
intricate fabric
up a gunslingers
sleeve...
Inside the
fine threads
of every lie
I weave...
Yeah...
inside the threads
of these lies
I weave...
Inside the
fine threads
of every lie
I tell...
Are the
go-to lines

I know
so well...
Like a
mushroomed bullet
or a gambler's
tell...
Inside the
fine threads
of every lie
I sell...
Yeah...
inside the threads
of these lies
I tell

TRAGIC BEAUTY IN SCARRED WORMWOOD

In a cedar
highboy
dresser...
next to
an album
from the
war...
We discovered
the sealed
blue envelope...
that held
his final
words...
They read —
Take
my body
back to
Brunswick...
n' lay me
to rest
on Hazel Ridge...
Then
mourn for me
no longer...

and forgive
those awful
things
I did...
I never
tried hard
to be
perfect...
n' usually
did the best
I could...
Yes...
this life's
been a
wild ride...
Tragic
beauty...
in
scarred
wormwood

MOURNING MOON

This
mourning
Moon
accentuates
the
timberline...
as
my
gin
soaked
eyes
play
tricks...

And
ancient
spirits
shape
shift...
beyond
the
orchard
bench
terraces...

Where
this
fresh
blood
trail
will
help
guide
them...
to
all
that's
left
of
me

HALF CRAZY

Bein'
half
crazy
is
still
fuckin'
nuts
and
those
who
know
me
best
already
understand...

I've
been
this
way
for
more
than
four
decades...

There's
no
prescription
pills...
potions
or
powders
made
to
save
me...

So
all
the
concerned
Christian
conservatives...

can
shove
those
sadistic
self-
help
books
up
their
self-
righteous
asses...

While
they
continue
to
spend
every
goddamn
day
just
prayin'
away
other
people's
sins....
because
it's
so
much
easier
to
perseverate...
than
deal
with
the
obvious
decay
dwellin'
deep
inside
themselves

KONNICHIWA & CAMERON CROWE

The night
I met
Matt Anderson
backstage
at Red
Square...
He
introduced
me to
a Hollywood
pimp...
that went
by the
name
Konnichiwa...

And
I stood
in awe...
when
I saw
him
flash
that fat
stack
of cash...

Just
moments
before...
the stage
door
flew open
and
Cameron
Crowe
strolled
through

HEROIN AT RED SQUARE

I could
feel fear
ridin' shotgun
inside my
big blown
pupils...

The night
I boosted
Sheri's
S-10 Chevy
and took it
South
to Tijuana...

Just so
I could see
Heroin
scream their
lungs out
one final time
at Red
Square

HAND GRENADES AT HOLY CROSS

The
night
ole
man
Murphy
got
arrested
for
attempted
murder...
he
had
five
LIVE
hand
grenades...

Stashed
away
safe...
in
an
organ
donor
cooler
he'd
swiped
from

a
transplant
team
at
Holy
Cross
Hospital...

And
nobody
on
the
South
Side....
ever
expected
to
see...

his
long
forgotten
face...
on
Channel
2
News
at
9pm

POOR MAN'S POLLOCK

At
3am...
I had
the need
to see
what a
hydra-shok
could do
to a can
of Allis
Chalmers
orange...

So
I placed
a case
of Krylon...
on the
regatta blue
trunk lid
of my
ex-wife's
'87 Ford
T-Bird...

Then let
my six
ninety six
dash two...
Leave
a poor
man's
Pollock...
And
an
I
owe
you

COLD HANDS IN THE BADLANDS

Here
in the
Badlands
of South
Dakota...
I'm no longer
intimidated
by the
illusion
of death
in my
rearview...

I'm just an
overoxidized
example
of what
flawed
men do...
when their
tortured trip
is almost
through...

Patiently
waitin' for
my shell
to be dissected...
by two cold
n' calloused
hands...
Of some
second-rate
medical
examiner
in Sioux Falls...
that probably
graduated
last in
his class...
the year
I was
born

CORN MASH MOONSHINE & MICKEY GILLEY
(For Grandpa Wayne)

In my
lever action
memory...

I can still
remember
the long
cold Winter
of '88...

When
we took
Dad's Scottsdale
out across
Roach Lake...

Listenin' to
Mickey Gilley
on 8-Track
tape...

While sippin'
corn mash
moonshine...
from an
ol' red
seven
bottle...

That Grandpa
had stashed
under the
tattered tan
bench seat
just six
weeks
before

SHANE'S '68 SKYLARK

When
we
discovered
Shane's
68
Buick
Skylark
abandoned
in
a
snow
drift
just
three
miles
West
of
Locust
Creek
Bridge...

I
was
goddamn
certain...
he'd
be
hurtin'
if

we
found
him...

Because
the
brutal
North
wind
had
cut
notches
in
my
exposed
skin...
And
despite
a
bright
Beaver
Moon
that
night...
even
the
hungriest
coyotes
were
too
cold
to
howl

ANOTHER YEAR OR TWO

The lonely
November night
Danny died
up in Detroit...
he was
still drivin'
that ole '63
split window
Stingray
we'd boosted
from a
cooked ass
bail bondsman
down in
Benton County
just three
months
before...

And
by the time
the Missouri
State Troopers
arrived at
my front
door...

I was
snorkelin'
off the coast
of Key Largo...
with Danny's
stepdaughter...
N' more
than enough
scratch
to stay
on the move...
for at least
another year
or two

LAST CALL FROM THE BAD LUCK BAR

It was a
bitter cold night
in late November...
when Danny
called me
from the
Bad Luck Bar
in Detroit...

I could barely
understand
his inebriated voice
through all the
background
noise...

He said
he'd grown
goddamn tired
of livin' life
on the run...
and that
he wouldn't
make it
to meet me
down in
Houston...

Because
he didn't
wanna die
in Texas
like his
Daddy did
back in the
fall of '83

GRACE

Sally
said
she
had
noticed
her
mother's
memory
was
fading
faster
last
Thanksgiving...

She
could
see
signs
of
pure
terror
hiding
behind
those
beautiful
china
blue
eyes...

It
haunted
Sally
every
night
for
six
long
months...
worryin'
about
her
mom's
rapid
decline...
And
what
it
must
feel
like...
to
be
trapped
inside
her
own
body...

As
Grace
escaped
into
a
final
fractured
midnight...
wearin'
her
favorite
champagne
headscarf
and
nothing
else

TAILWIND

In
this
wild-
eyed
windshield
reflection
I
see
my
aging
expression
starin'
back
at
me
in
solemn
disbelief...
I
wonder
how
in
the
hell
I

survived
so
long...

Knowin'
all
too
well...
this
road
worn
shell...
will
carry
me
as
far
as
the
tailwind
takes
me

PINOT LIPS

VERSE I

She said —
*I need
the kind
of man...
that knows
which moves
to use...
The
in between
damn obscene...
low down
dirty blues....*

CHORUS:

Come on...
n' give me
somethin'
wicked...
Baby...
show me
your twisted
tricks...
Oh...

tell me lies...
with those
cocaine eyes...
n' taste my
pinot lips...
Yeah...
taste these
pinot lips

VERSE II

She said —
Evil is
all I
need
right now...
closed casket
and an
open bar...
Five
white lines...
two magnums
of wine...
and a faster
getaway car...
Yeah...a faster
getaway car

REPEAT CHORUS (Twice)

AFTERBURNERS GLOW

On
a
neon
soaked
sidewalk
in
the
Spring
of
'91...
we
met
Sherri
standin'
in
line....
while
waitin'
to
ride
the
Giant
Dipper...

She
had
three

silver
dollar
sized
bleach
stains...
strategically
splashed
down
her
left
Levi's
leg...
and
a
Bad
Radio
bootleg
t-shirt

she
swore
Eddie
Vedder
had
refused
to
sign
the
night
before...

Sherri
looked
like
Alicia
Silverstone's
sexier
half
sister
and
was
certainly
more
well
read
than
anyone
else
we'd
met
so
far
in
San
Diego....

It
was
the
first
of
many
nights

we'd
meet
on
Mission
Beach...
just
to
talk
shit
about
local
bands
and
get
stoned
while
watchin'
the
afterburners
glow
low
over
the
Pacific

SCRAPS OF OUR HELLBOUND SOULS

We were
somehow
sewn together...
like bloody
fingers severed
on an antique
butcher's block...

Just three
lost thieves
from Kansas City...

Willin'
to risk
everything...
because the fear
of havin'
nothin' again...
never scared us
quite enough...
to give it all up
for the sake
of savin'
the scraps
of our
hellbound
souls

CHRYSLER AVENUE

Inside
this
sky
blue
mornin'...
I'm
reminded
of
the
time
my
friend
Tony
called
me
from
his
deathbed...

He
just
wanted
to
say
he
was

sorry
and
there
was
no
need
to
worry...

Because
the
scratch
we
stole...
was
still
stashed
in
the
trunk

of
his
Brother's
'76
Eldorado....

Parked
inside
an
abandoned
warehouse...
just
a
mile
South
of
where
we
made
our
final
score
off
Chrysler
Avenue

ROOM 206

I
had
to
stop
wantin'
it...

When
the
pain
was
too
much
to
bear...

Just
sittin'
alone
my
motel
room...

Gettin'
high
in
an
easy
chair...

Yeah...
I
had
to
stop
wantin'
it...

Outta
scratch...
n'
still
needin'
a
fix...

Oh...
I
had
to
stop
wantin'
it...

At
the
Desert
Hills
in
room
206

OUTSIDE THOSE STATIC LINES

Sometimes
I
stop
n'
study
the
exhausted
eyes...
of
a
man
I
no
longer
recognize...
Knowin'
he's
barely
gettin'
by...
outside
those
static
lines...

Where
a
paranoid
scowl...
refuses
surrender
somehow...
Just
to
allow
him
enough
time...
to
rewrite
his
final
obituary
in
disappearing
ink

GORY DETAILS

In September
of '86...
Scary Larry
McGreggor
buried three
greedy bankers...
just eight miles
Southeast of
Birch Tree
Missouri...

N' while
their bodies
were never
discovered...
ole Larry
kept his
bases
covered...

Until lung
cancer
caught up
with him
and he
confessed

all the
gory details
from a
morphine drip
deathbed...
in room
number
twelve
at the
Las
Palmas
Hotel
in
Hollywood

THOMPSON GUN

Verse I

I shook hands
with death
again
yesterday
And told
him twice
he should
stay away...
But
he failed
to listen...
on Boxing Day
So I
planted him
shallow
in an
unmarked
grave —

CHORUS-

I'm raggedy
n' mean...

like a hound
on the run
And a real
motherfucker
with this
Thompson gun
Yeah...
I'm a real
motherfucker
with this
Thompson gun

Verse II

I bluffed
the reaper
again
tonight
And told
him twice
how I love
to fight
N' with
big brass
knuckles
I turned
out his
lights

Then
buried him
deep
neath the
Wolf Moon
bright —

REPEAT CHORUS (Twice)

THE TENDERLOIN ROOM

We
sat
there
alone
in
the
Tenderloin
Room
at
the
Chase
Park
Plaza
in
Saint
Louis...

Sippin'
on
Oban
eighteen...
just
tryin'
to
gain

the
strength
to
believe...

In
the
kind
of
things
only
dyin'
men
do
when
they
wake
up
feelin'
desperate

TRIAL HORSE

I'm an old
trial horse...
still takin'
the stage...
Circlin' inside
the ropes...
where a
microphone hangs...
If you're here
for some action
I've got more
than you'll need...

I'm an old
trial horse
With new tricks
up my sleeve...
Yeah...
I'm the old
trial horse
I've got
tricks up
my sleeve —

I'm an old
trial horse
in total
control...
Tape
over gauze
with a
brawler's nose

There's bookies...
and junkies
bettin' big
against me...
Oh...
I'm the old
trial horse...
they love
watchin'
me bleed
Yeah...
I'm the old
trial horse...
n' they
pay me
to bleed

FIGHTING COCK & ROLLING ROCK

I was
beyond
desperate
n' tryin' hard
to stretch
sixty eight
dollars
until my next
commission check
could be cut
the followin'
Friday...

I'd been
livin' thin
for a
few months
by then...
dinin' on
Van Camp's
Pork n' Beans...
and three
sleeves
of stale
Saltines...

Thirsty for
better bourbon...
but willin'
to settle
for a fifth
of Fighting
Cock
and an
imperfect
case of
Rolling
Rock...
that a
delivery
driver
dropped
in the
Kwik Shop
parkin' lot...

just around
the corner
from my
shitty one
bedroom
apartment
and rabbit
ear foil
antenna
TV

EZINE ANXIETIES

We're
just
a
sleep
away
from
the
First
Annual
Ezine
Awards
at
Under
The
Bleachers...

So
I'm
writin'
this
long
winded
acceptance
speech...
in
an

attempt
to
demonstrate
how
goddamn
humble
I
really
am...

I know...
I know...

How
do
I
expect
to
win...
when
I've
never
even
been
nominated
for
a
Pushcart
Prize...

And
when
will
I
begin to
realize...
that
I'm
not
really
popular
enough
to
win
an
Ezine
anyway...

Ya
know...
I'd
rather
be
Susan
Fuckin'
Lucci
of
the
Ezines...
than
feel

the
need
to
campaign
for
my
name
to
be
included
among
the
best
of
the
best
of
the
better
than
the
rest...

Let' em
all
think
they're
better...
I
say

CHAIN SMOKIN' DEATHBED

In
December
of
'95...
we
were
hired
by
The
Partnership
to
run
guns
from
Detroit
down
to
West
Memphis...

Which
worked
fine...
more
than
a
few
times...

Until
they
tried
to
clip
us
twice
on
Christmas
Eve...

While
Dean
Martin
was
barely
clingin'
to
life...
still
chain
smokin'
Kent
cigarettes...
in
his
deathbed
off

North
Maple
Drive
in
Beverly
Hills

ASSASSIN'S TOUPEE

When
Seth
cheated
death
for
the
final
time
in
West
Memphis...

A
hollow
eyed
hitman...
unmasked
just
long
enough
to
ask
if
he
had
any
last
requests...

As
Seth
pulled
a
double
barrel
Derringer
from
his
left
hip
pocket...

N'
painted
the
rose
pink
Frigidaire
with
high
velocity
spatter...
gray
matter...
and
tufts
of
the
assassin's
toupee

BLUESMEN IN BUFFALO

Lucky
says
the
first
time
he
jammed
with
Willie
Dixon
at
Governor's
Inn...

He'd
just
turned
five
the
week
before...

And
was
known
to

be
better
than
half
the
goddamn
bluesmen
in
Buffalo
already

HOW THIS TRIP ENDS

I
already
know
how
this
trip
ends...
With
three
rifle
volleys
and
a
few
fickle
friends...

My
funeral
flag
folded...
thirteen
times...
Handed
to
an
angel...
that
used

to
be
mine —

I
already
know
how
this
trip
ends...

Like
a
well
worn
watch...
that
time
made
thin...

Mascara
soaked
lace...
and
my
ashes
in
the
wind...

Oh...
I
already
know
how
this
trip
ends...

Cause
I've
been
here
before...
n'
I'll
be
back
again...

Yeah...
I
already
know
how
this
trip
ends

INCONSEQUENTIAL

When
chickenshit
Vincent
called
to
say
he
was
sorry
if
his
words
were
offensive...

I
told
him
I
was
never
really
hip
to
his
jive
to
begin
with...

So
his
words
were
already
deemed
inconsequential

SUNRISE ON KO SAMUI

In
his
final
days...
Diamond
Dave...
lived
in
a
double-
wide
down
by
Round
Grove
Creek...

And
that
ole
grizzled
son
of
a
bitch...
would
go

for
weeks
without
sleep...

Souped
up
on
bathtub
speed...
just
tryin'
to
make
enough
to
take
him
back

to
see
the
sunrise
on
Ko
Samui

ANOTHER SUNRISE

Behind
a
pale
purple
privacy
curtain
at
Mount
Sinai...

I
could
hear
an
exhausted
triage
nurse
say...

He might
be among
the walkin'
wounded
right now...

But
if we
let him
leave...
he'll never
survive
long
enough
to see
the
sunrise
over
Lake
Michigan
again

RHODE ISLAND RED

Rhode
Island
Red
always
said —

*There's really
no use
in lyin'
to a dyin'
man....
He won't
have
enough
energy
to fight
the truth
anyway*

JOHNNY'S LAST RIDE

When
Johnny
boosted
that
sapphire
blue
Escalade
from
Robbins
Salvage
in
Oskaloosa...

He
didn't
expect
the
local
law
would
track
him
down...

Before
he
could
make
it
back
to
Tony's
chop
shop...
just
two
miles
South
of
Meriden

PREFERRED RENDEZVOUS

We
were
runnin'
smooth
in
the
groove
and
on
the
outskirts
of
out
of
control...

Ramblin'
South
in
my
'96
Eldorado....

Poppin'
little
pink
pills
n'

washin'
them
down
with
a
fractured
fifth
of
Evan
Williams…

Tryin'
to
stay
awake
long
enough…
to
make
it
to
our
preferred
rendezvous
point…
just
East
of
Kimberling
City

PEACOCKIN' POET FROM POUGHKEEPSIE

There's a
part-time poet
from Poughkeepsie
that started
trollin' me
about six
months ago...

And since
the snarky
old bastard
is way too
fuckin' slow...
to disrupt
my elusive flow...

He keeps
himself busy...
postin' cryptic
notes...
N' peacockin'
out in front
of folks...

Tellin' them
how he
plans to
clip me
up on stage
someday...

Long before
my words
can corrupt
the imaginary
masses...

N'
I just have
to laugh

as I read
the best
of my
unpublished
work
to another
empty room...

Because any
half-assed
assassin
knows...
there's
really
no use
in killin'
a man
that's
dead
inside
already

HAWK FLOP TSUNAMI

In the
early mornin'
moments of
Boxing Day
2004...
I watched
a wounded
Cooper's hawk
flop for
half an hour...

Before
shootin'
him
in the
head...
with a
sawed-off
single shot
sixteen...

And as
a local
radio DJ
interrupted

*Live like
you were dyin...*
Just
long enough
to report the
deadliest
Tsunami
in recent
world history....

I continued
to ignore
my own
mortality...
while loadin'
that ol'
shotgun
again

Americana songwriter and Kansas-City-based storyteller K.W. Peery is the author of eight poetry collections: *Tales of a Receding Hairline; Purgatory; Wicked Rhythm; Ozark Howler; Gallatin Gallows; Howler Holler; Bootlegger's Bluff; Cockpit Chronicles.* He is founder and co-editor of The *Angel's Share Literary Magazine* (Shine Runner Press). His work is included in the Vincent Van Gogh Anthology *Resurrection of a Sunflower, The Cosmic Lost and Found:*

An Anthology of Missouri Poets (Spartan Press), *Best of Mad Swirl Anthology 2018* and the Walsall Poetry Society Anthology, *Diverse Verse II & III*. Credited as a lyricist and producer, Peery's work appears on more than twenty studio albums over the past decade. Website: www.kwpeery.com

This project was made possible, in part, by generous support from the Osage Arts Community.

Osage Arts Community provides temporary time, space and support for the creation of new artistic works in a retreat format, serving creative people of all kinds — visual artists, composers, poets, fiction and nonfiction writers. Located on a 152-acre farm in an isolated rural mountainside setting in Central Missouri and bordered by ¾ of a mile of the Gasconade River, OAC provides residencies to those working alone, as well as welcoming collaborative teams, offering living space and workspace in a country environment to emerging and mid-career artists. For more information, visit us at www.osageac.org

www.ingramcontent.com/pod-product-compliance
Lightning Source LLC
Chambersburg PA
CBHW030111100526
44591CB00009B/370